THE INDEPEND

UNIVERSAL HOLLYWOOD 2020

G. COSTA

A Special Thanks

Thank you very much for purchasing *The Independent Guide to Universal Studios Hollywood 2020*. We hope this guide makes a big difference to your trip and you have found some tips that will save you time, money and hassle.

To get in touch, please use the 'Contact Us' form on our website at www.independentguidebooks.com/contact-us/. You can also sign up to our newsletter on our website (on the right sidebar).

If you have enjoyed this guide you will want to check out:

- The Independent Guide to Disneyland
- The Independent Guide to Universal Orlando
- The Independent Guide to Walt Disney World
- The Independent Guide to Disneyland Paris
- The Independent Guide to Paris
- The Independent Guide to New York City
- The Independent Guide to Tokyo
- The Independent Guide to Hong Kong
- The Independent Guide to London

Our theme park travel guides give you detailed information on every ride, show and attraction and more insider tips that will save you hours in line! Our city guides are great overviews of cities with top attractions, good places to eat and stay, explanations of the transport system and much more.

All that's left to say is: have fun at Universal Studios Hollywood!

Photo credits:
The following photos have been used in this guide under a Creative Commons attribution 2.0 license:

Universal globe (cover) – Miguel Discart; Tram (cover), and Jurassic Park Splashdown (cover) – Jeremy Thompson; Animal Actors and Waterworld (cover) – William Warby; Universal Globe (inside) – Prayitno; WaterWorld – Sebi Ryffel; The Simpsons Ride – distillated; Inside-Universal Globe - Mathieu Marquer; Tickets - Chris Schmich; Trolley Show - 'furlong'; vertical tram - Rojer; Despicable Me Minion Mayhem, Shrimp meal, VIP Experience, Potter Dancers and Jurassic Park/World- 'Prayitno'; Universal's Animal Actors - Daryl Mitchell; The Walking Dead Attraction and The Three Broomsticks - Jeremy Thompson; Harry Potter & the Forbidden Journey and Disneyland Hotel - Harshlight; Hogsmeade Shop - Ruth Hartnup; Universal Characters Show and iFly Skydiving - Loren Javier; CityWalk - Ana Paula Hirama; Quick Service Food and Kwik-e-mart - Miguel Discart; Mummy ride facade - 'winnieatcolby'; Studio tour set - 'CKGolf'

Other photo credits: Hilton and The Garland- Time Out; Loews - Travelzoo; Marriott Burbank and Sportsmen's Lodge Hotel- Booking.com. Some photos © Universal.

Contents

Introduction

Welcome to The Independent Guide to Universal Studios Hollywood 2020. This travel guide will take you through the entire process of visiting Universal Studios in Hollywood, California from choosing a hotel, to insights into every attraction, and even ways to save time in queue lines.

Universal Studios Hollywood (often abbreviated to USH herein) is the ninth most popular theme park in the USA, with over 9 million visitors in 2014. However, comparing it to other theme parks is a bit unfair – USH is not just a theme park but a real working film studio going back over 100 years.

Even since opening day in 1915, the studio offered tours of the sets and backlots. In 1930, however, when movies with sound came about, the tour had to be discontinued as guests were disrupting production.

In 1964, the theme park experience opened with a revamped Studio Tour. Ever since attractions have been added, the Studio Tour has been expanded, and the theme park attracts more visitors than ever before.

In total, the theme park now houses 15 attractions, shows and other experiences, and there is constant innovation.

So, let's get into it!

Tickets

Getting the right Universal Studios Hollywood ticket is crucial, and it can save you a lot of money. There are several different ticket options to consider.

All About Tickets

Guests from any country can buy advanced tickets. The easiest place to purchase these is the official Universal Studios Hollywood website at *universalstudios hollywood.com*.

Guests who do not buy their tickets in advance can do so at the theme parks, but prices are higher.

Ticket Types:
There are main types of tickets: a Single Day or Multi-Day ticket, and an annual or season pass.

Child prices apply to children aged 3 to 9 years old. Children under 3 get free admission into the theme parks (proof of age

may be requested on entry).

Tickets bought via Universal's official website gives you savings of $10 to $30 compared to purchasing the tickets at the theme park, plus you get early

park admission into the Wizarding World of Harry Potter area of the park.

Getting your tickets:
Advanced Tickets will be emailed to you and must be printed before arrival.

General Admission:

	Low	Mid	High	Peak	Super-Peak	2-Day
Adult	$109	$114	$119	$124	$129	$149-$169
Child	$103	$108	$113	$118	$123	$143-$163

To buy a general admission ticket, when booking you must choose a date for your visit. For 2-day tickets, you must select the date of your first visit - the second visit must be used within seven days of the first visit.

Anytime Admission:

These tickets allow you to visit the theme park on any day you want and are priced at $139 per adult and $133 per child.

By visiting the Universal Studios Hollywood website and simulating a ticket purchase, you can check which price bracket your tickets will fall into. Advanced purchase general admission tickets are always cheaper than tickets bought on the day itself at the theme park.

Universal Express

A Universal Express ticket allows access to Universal Studios Hollywood theme park for one day, and front of the line access to each attraction once, as well as priority seating at each show. Pricing is the same for each guest aged over 3. Prices below are for advanced purchases - if buying at the gate, add $10 to each ticket.

	Low Season	Mid Season	High Season	Peak Season
Price	$179 to $189	$199 to $219	$229 to $239	$249 to $259

Annual Passes

Annual passes allow you to visit Universal Studios Hollywood as often as you wish (subject to blackout dates on some passes) at a low per-visit price. In addition, exclusive perks are on offer to Passholders including discounts on dining and merchandise.

	Silver Annual Pass	Gold Annual Pass	Platinum Annual Pass
Price	$189	$319	$619
A Year of Unlimited Admission	No. Over 275 days are available for entry,	No. Over 330 days are available for entry,	Yes. Entry every day of the year.
Free Parking	No	Yes	Yes
Discounted theme park and HHN tickets	Yes	Yes	Yes
One free Halloween Horror Nights ticket	No	No	Yes
Invitations to annual pass preview events	No	Yes	Yes
Discounted food, merchandise and speciality items	No	Yes (15%)	Yes (15%)
10-20% discount at certain CityWalk locations	Yes	Yes	Yes
Universal Express Access to all rides, shows and attractions	No	No	Yes

Passes are valid for one year. Prices are the same for all guests regardless of age. A $10 discount is available for all passes purchased online.

Top Tip: If you are planning two visits to the park within 365 days, an annual pass can be a real bargain if the blackout dates work for you - you can check these online.

Getting There

Before all the fun begins at Universal Studios Hollywood, you must first get there.

By Car

Universal Studios Hollywood is a 10-mile drive from downtown Los Angeles along the US-101 N. In light traffic this takes about 15 minutes, whereas at peak times it can take 45 minutes.

There are five parking areas. In order of proximity, they are: Frankenstein (Front Gate Parking - closest), Woody Woodpecker (Preferred Parking), Jurassic Park (Preferred Parking), Curious George, and the furthest is E.T.

Except for the Frankenstein lot, which is by the park entrance, you will walk from the other parking lots to the CityWalk entertainment area, and then to the theme park entrance itself.

The furthest garage is about a 15 to 20-minute walk from your car to the park, whereas the closest is less than a 5-minute walk.

General parking is $25, preferred parking is $35, and front gate parking is $50. Discounts operate for arrivals after 6:00 pm.

From Disneyland Resort: Many visitors to Universal Studios Hollywood also spend time at the Disneyland Resort. The resorts are located on opposite sides of Los Angeles (35-miles apart) with a travel time of between 1 hour and 1 hour 30 minutes by car. From Disneyland Resort you take the I-5 North, joining the US-101 North just outside downtown L.A.

Public Transportation

From Los Angeles International Airport (LAX): From LAX, take the LAX FlyAway bus to Hollywood/Vine Station (buses depart hourly, journey time is about 1 hour). At Hollywood/Vine, take the subway (Metro Red Line) to Universal City Station, where you get a complimentary shuttle bus to Universal Studios Hollywood. The total journey time is about 1 hour 30 minutes, costing $9.75.

From Downtown LA: Universal City station is located on the subway Metro Red Line. Travel time from Union Station in Downtown LA to Universal City station is about 25 minutes. You can get a TAP card for use on the Metro at a machine at the station for $1 and then add credit. A one-way trip is $1.75. At Universal City station, take the free official shuttle bus.

From Disneyland Resort: First, take the 15 bus from the Disneyland Main Transportation Center to ARTIC (a transport hub including the bus station and Anaheim Station for trains). The journey is about 15 to 20 minutes.

Once at ARTIC/Anaheim Station, you can either take the Pacific Surfliner Amtrak train (a long-distance service) or the Metrolink Orange County Line (a regional service) into L.A. Union Station. This will take about 45 minutes.

At Union Station in downtown L.A., get the Metro Red Line to 'Universal/Studio City Station'. Then get the shuttle bus up to the theme park. This is a 25 minute trip on the Metro, plus 5 to 20 minutes for the shuttle, depending on the wait.

The total journey time for the trip, including waiting, is 2 hours 30 minutes to 3 hours 30 minutes. Visit metro.net to plan. The total cost is about $25. You need exact change for the bus.

Check the schedule for the train part of your trip to avoid being stranded in L.A. on return as services end early in the day. At the time of writing, the last train leaves L.A. Union Station on weekdays at 6:40 pm and on weekends at 4:40 pm. These trains are also infrequent.

If travelling in a group, we recommend making this journey by taxi - it is quicker, simpler and cheaper.

Hotels

Many hotels are available near Universal Studios Hollywood, and you are free to choose from the hundreds on offer in both the Hollywood area, downtown L.A. or further afield.

None of these hotels are operated by Universal itself; these are partner hotels. This means that you can book these hotels as part of a Universal package with tickets and the hotel together, which may save you money and time - hotels booked with a vacation package also allow you early entry into the theme park. Room prices shown below are for a weekday off-peak date in November 2019. Rates during peak seasons are higher.

Hilton Los Angeles - Universal City

This 495-room hotel is the closest to the theme park with walking paths to the park and CityWalk (5-minute walk) or you can use the complimentary shuttle.

Transportation: On-site. Free shuttle service. Can walk to Universal Studios in 5 minutes.

Room prices: From $275 for a standard room.

Amenities: Convenience store, business center, café, fitness center, outdoor pool, in-room dining, and Wi-Fi.

This 4-star hotel is ideally located just a 5-minute walk away from the theme park, or you can use the complimentary shuttle. The metro station is less than a 10-minute walk.

Although pricey compared to some other options, you are paying for the excellent location and attention to service here. The outdoor pool, in particular, is excellent. Wi-Fi is an extra charge at this hotel. Parking is $28 per day ($40 for valet).

Sheraton Universal

This 457-room hotel is very close to the theme park with walking paths to the park and CityWalk (10-minute walk) or you can use the complimentary shuttle.

Transportation: On-site. Free shuttle service. Can walk to Universal Studios in 10 minutes.

Room size: 325 ft² for a traditional guest room

Room prices: From $238 for a standard room

Amenities: Business center, fitness center, outdoor pool, in-room dining, and Wi-Fi.

Like the Hilton, the 4-star Sheraton is located on-site at Universal and is about 10-minutes' walk to the theme park, slightly further than the Hilton. Also known as the "Hotel of the Stars",

customers are the number one priority at this hotel. As well as standard rooms, suites are also available at this hotel.

Wi-Fi is an extra charge, but it is complimentary for loyalty club members.

Parking is $30 per day ($45 for valet).

The Garland

This 257-room hotel is suited for those looking for a base convenient for both Hollywood and the theme park, yet away from the hustle and bustle.

Transportation: Trolley service to Universal Studios

Room prices: From $272 for a standard room

Amenities: Wi-Fi, on-site restaurant and lounge, fitness center, outdoor pool, business center and valet parking.

This boutique hotel offers luxury just minutes from Universal Studios. Live the Hollywood lifestyle in this charming, retro-chic accommodation.
A trolley service connects the hotel with Universal Studios Hollywood and the metro station in just five minutes; you can also walk to nearby restaurants.

Free Wi-Fi is available at this hotel.

Loews Hollywood Hotel

This 628-room hotel is suited for those wishing to stay in Hollywood surrounded by the glitz and glamour instead of the theme park area.

Transportation: 1-stop away on the metro

Room size: 400 ft² for a standard room

Room prices: From $369 for a standard room

Amenities: Outdoor pool, full-service spa, fitness center, in-room dining and business center.

Located in Hollywood itself, and 1-minute from Hollywood Boulevard, the 4-star Loews Hollywood Hotel is the perfect location for seeing the stars.

What's more, the hotel is just one stop on the metro from Universal Studios Hollywood – the total journey time from the hotel to the theme park is a mere 18 minutes. Complimentary Wi-Fi is available.

Los Angeles Marriott Burbank Airport

Convenient for those flying into Burbank Airport, this hotel is located a 5-mile, 15-minute drive away from the theme park.

Transportation: Complimentary scheduled shuttle service to Universal Studios. Must be reserved.

Number of rooms: 488

Room prices: Standard rooms from $338 per night

Amenities: On-site restaurant, outdoor pool, Wi-Fi, fitness center, valet parking and business center

Located right by Burbank airport, this 4-star hotel is convenient for anyone looking to stay a bit further out and be based by the airport.

A complimentary scheduled shuttle service to Universal Studios Hollywood and the airport is available, although reservations are required. Wi-Fi is charged but loyalty program members can get it for free.

Sportsmen's Lodge Hotel

The most unique hotel in the line-up, those wanting a trendy and budget-friendly place to stay need look no further.

Transportation: Complimentary shuttle service

Number of rooms: 190

Room size: 300 ft^2 for a traditional guest room

Room prices: Standard rooms from $199 per night

Amenities: Wi-Fi, on-site restaurant and lounge, outdoor pool and business center.

A unique combination of rustic, San Fernando Valley charm and Tinseltown polish, the 3-star Sportsmen Lodge Hotel is just minutes away from the action of Universal Studios Hollywood by complimentary shuttle.

This was once a haven for movie stars in the '50s, '60s and '70s.

Wi-Fi is complimentary. There is no fitness suite at this hotel, but the pool is the largest in the San Fernando Valley.

Park Guide

Universal Studios Hollywood is a relatively small theme park with fewer than twenty attractions in total. Due to space constraints, however, the attraction selection is strong. As the park is small, you should be able to complete it in one day comfortably.

Note: Average attraction waits noted in this section are estimates for busy summer days and on school breaks. Wait times may be lower at other times of the year. They may also occasionally be higher, especially during the weeks of 4th July, Thanksgiving, Christmas, New Year and other public holidays.

Where we list food prices, this information was accurate during our last visit to the restaurant. We also do not post the full menu but just a sample of the food on offer. Meal prices listed do not include a drink, unless otherwise stated. When an attraction is listed as requiring lockers, all loose items must be stored in complimentary lockers outside the attraction.

Park Entrance:
The park entrance area is the gateway to Universal Studios Hollywood. You pass through it on the way in and out.

This area is where Guest Relations is located where you can get help with disability passes, questions, positive feedback and complaints. Guest Relations is located to the right-hand side after the turnstiles. This area also has locker rentals, as well as stroller and wheelchair rentals.

First Aid is located along the Upper Lot area next to the theater housing *Animal Actors*. Another First Aid station is located near *Jurassic World: The Ride.*

Attraction Key

In the next two chapters, we list each attraction individually along with some key information. Here is a key to the symbols in the following sections.

🎟️	Does it have Express Pass?	📏	Minimum height (in inches)
📷	Is there an On-Ride Photo?	⌄	Ride/Show Length
⌛	Average wait times (on peak days)		
🔒	Do I need to place my belongings in a locker before riding?		

Upper Lot

The Upper Lot is the main part of the theme park and contains the entrance and many of the park's attractions. This area is also directly connected to Wizarding World of Harry Potter. At the end of the Upper Lot, you will find escalators and elevators (dubbed 'The StarWay') taking you down to the Lower Lot and the attractions located there.

Attractions

Despicable Me Minion Mayhem

| 🎟 Yes | 40" | 📷 No | ✓ 4 minutes | 🔒 No | ⏳ 60 to 120 minutes |

A simulator ride featuring 4D effects and the characters from Despicable Me.

Due to the low hourly capacity and the popularity of its characters, queues are almost always lengthy, but they are shortest early in the morning as it is not very visible from the main park walkways.

Top Tip: A stationary version of this attraction operates with benches at the front of the theater which do not move, but you still get the 3D experience. When this is offered, the wait time is usually short, e.g. 10 minutes versus 90 minutes. There is a separate queue line for this.

Height Restriction: Guests under 40" (1.02m) may not ride. Those between 40" and 48" (1.22m) must ride accompanied. Guests over 48" may ride alone.

Super Silly Fun Land

Height Restriction: 48 inches (1.22m) maximum
Average Wait: None. Walkthrough and play area
Express Pass: No
Lockers Required: No

Based on a seaside funfair from the Despicable Me films, this play area is split into two parts – a dry playground and a water-filled play area. There are changing rooms available for visitors to change into swimwear if they wish. This is an open area of the park, with no queue lines.

Silly Swirly

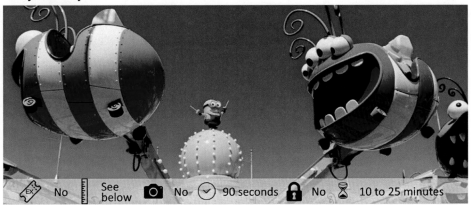

No	See below	No	90 seconds	No	10 to 25 minutes

This is a reasonably standard fairground style ride that is part of Super Silly Fun Land.

It is similar to the Dumbo rides at Disney parks. Here you sit in a bug and go around in a circle; you can control the height of your bug using a joystick inside the vehicle.

As it is so hidden away, waits usually stay under 10 minutes, possibly peaking at 25 minutes on very busy days.

Height Restriction: 48" (1.22m) minimum to ride alone. Riders under 48" must be accompanied by someone aged 14 or older.

Kung-Fu Panda Adventure

Yes	None	No	8 minutes	No	Less than 15 minutes

Stepping into *Kung-Fu Panda Adventure*, you know you are getting into a different kind of attraction. The unique part of this attraction is the seats, which act like personal simulators.

For those not wishing to experience the seat movement, a limited number of stationary seats are also available.

The movie is great fun with typical Dreamworks humor, and character fans are unlikely to be disappointed.

The run-time of 8 minutes includes both the main show and the pre-show.

The Secret Life of Pets: Off the Leash! (Opens 2020)

Opening in 2020, Universal has released very few details regarding this upcoming attraction.

As such the best description we have of the ride comes from deadline.com: "The ride will blend live, dimensional and animated characters with what the park calls "hyper-realistic media" as guests zip along a track aboard ride vehicles. Their path will go through bustling New York City streets towards the pet adoption event and their ultimate arrival in a home. Along the way will pop up an array of challenges and fellow animals."

WaterWorld

Yes	None	No	20 minutes	No	At scheduled times

Despite being based on one of Hollywood's biggest flops, *WaterWorld* is constantly rated as the best show in the park by visitors.

This stunt show features a whole load of pyrotechnics, fire, water effects and many surprises throughout. Action fans are sure to be in for a treat!

Beware of the wet zone, where you will get splashed a fair few times.

The auditorium for this show is the largest in the park, but *WaterWorld* is also a very popular choice; be in the queue at least 15 minutes before show time to get a seat.

Special Effects Show
Show Length: 20 to 25 minutes
Express Pass: Yes
Lockers Required: No

This is one of our favourite shows at the park, featuring a fun and educational insight into how special effects and stunts are used in the making of movies. The show is a great laugh, and if you are in the queue line early enough, you may even be cast to participate, if you wish. You generally do not need to arrive at the theater any earlier than 15 minutes before the show begins, as there are a large number of seats.

The Simpsons Ride

Yes | See below | Yes | 5 minutes | No | 45 to 90 minutes

The Simpsons Ride brings the famous yellow Springfield family to life in a fun-filled simulator-style ride in front of an enormous screen - in this experience, you enter Krustyland and ride a wild simulated roller coaster.

Your adventure is filled with gags throughout and is a fun family experience. Simpsons fans will love this ride!

Height Restriction: Guests under 40 inches (1.02m) may not ride. Those between 40 inches and 48 inches (1.22m) must ride accompanied. Guests over 48 inches may ride alone.

Universal's Animal Actors

Yes | None | No | 20 minutes | No | At scheduled times

A behind-the-scenes look at how animals are taught to act in films, including audience participation.

It is not our favourite show in the park, but animal fans will enjoy this.

You will not need to generally turn up more than fifteen minutes in advance to secure a spot as this is not a hugely popular show, although animal fans should be sure not to miss this.

Universal Studio Tour

Yes | None | No | 45 to 60 minutes | No | 40 to 75 minutes

The park's star attraction, the Universal Studio Tour is the reason that the theme park was founded.

Well before USH was a theme park, the Studio Tour operated as a single attraction, allowing guests to visit parts of Universal's studios. Now, it is one of several attractions in the park, but remains hugely popular and is one of the main reasons why many guests visit the theme park.

The ride takes place in huge trams, with rows seating six people. The trams take you on a non-stop tour lasting between 45 and 60 minutes. The exact length of this experience depends on access conditions and whether all segments of the tour are operational. A live guide narrates the experience, and a TV personality appears on screens in the trams once in a while to add more detail.

On some sections of the tour, you pass soundstages

and other sets used for production, whereas other parts of the journey have mini attractions that have been created exclusively for the tram tour, such as the immersive 360-degree experience starring King Kong.

Every few years, a section of the tour changes. Current sets include:

Colonial Street (Wisteria Lane), The Front Lot, Little Europe, Metropolitan New York Sets, The Old West (Six Points Texas), War of the Worlds and Whoville.

As well as the sets, there are the following staged action events throughout the tour: Jurassic Park, Old Mexico: Flash Flood, JAWS, Earthquake: The Big One, Psycho: Bates Motel, KONG 360 and Fast & Furious: Supercharged.

We will not go into any more detail as to what happens in each of these segments to maintain an air

of surprise. Some sections of the tour are intense, and there is a chance you may get wet.

You should expect wait times for this attraction to build up very quickly, from park opening, peaking in the early afternoon.

As the tour is such a complex logistical operation, it closes earlier than the rest of the park. The last tour generally departs 1 hour 40 minutes before park closing, though the exact timing will be displayed at the attraction entrance and wait time signs throughout the park.

Tours are in English, though there are also tours in Spanish and Mandarin available at select times. Check the in-park guide for the timing of these.

A VIP Tour option is also available. More details later in this guide.

The Walking Dead Attraction

Yes	None	No	3 minutes	No	15 to 30 minutes

This attraction is a permanent haunted house experience allowing horror fans to experience what it would be like to enter the world of AMC's Walking Dead as they attempt to escape the zombie apocalypse.

Even though there are no height restrictions, as this is a scare maze the experience is unsuitable for children - there are scareactors, loud sounds, flashing lighting and other startling scenes.

DINING

Springfield U.S.A. Restaurants:
• **Bumblebee Man's Taco Truck** sells tacos, nachos and beer. Entrees are $10-$13.
• **Cletus' Chicken Shack** sells fried chicken, salads and chicken sandwiches. Entrees are $12-$16.
• **Duff Brewery Beer Garden** sells refreshing Duff beer and light bar snacks.
• **Krusty Burger** sells burgers, hot dogs and Buzz Cola.
• **Lard Lad's Donuts** sells donuts and coffee. Large donuts are $7.50, drinks are $3-$5.
• **Luigi's Pizza** sells personal-sized pizzas. Entrees are priced at $9.50-$13.
• **Moe's Tavern** sells Flaming Moes and Duff Beer, as well as light bar snacks.
• **Phineas Q. Butterfat's Ice Cream** sells ice creams and sundaes. Ice creams are $7.
• **Sud McDuff's Hot Dogs** sells hot dogs, pretzels, churros and more. Snacks are $5-$11.

Cinnabon – Serves cinnamon rolls, ice cream, coffee and other drinks. Rolls are $6-$9.
Cocina Mexicana – Serves Mexican fare inclduing tacos and burritos. Entrees are $13.
Despicable Delights – Serves popcorn, smoothies, fruit, and more. Snacks are $5-$8.
French Street Bistro – Serves sandwiches, salads, and pastries. Entrees are $11-$13.
Gru's Lab Café – Serves nachos, rotisserie chicken, sandwiches and salads. Entrees are $12-$16.
Hollywood & Dine – Serves burgers, sandwiches and pizzas. Entrees are $12-$14.
Mel's Diner – Serves burgers, sandwiches, pies and milkshakes. Entrees are $13-$14.
Mulligan's Pub & Spirits – A pub serving alcoholic and non-alcoholic drinks. Alcoholic drinks are $12-$15.
Palace Theatre Café – Serves sandwiches, salads, turkey legs, rotisserie chicken, burritos and soups. Operates seasonally. Entrees are $11-$13.

The Wizarding World of Harry Potter

Step into the world of Harry Potter and experience what it is like to visit Hogsmeade. Dine, visit the shops and experience the fantastic rides.

The Wizarding World is by far the best-themed area of the theme park, and Potter fans will see authenticity unlike anywhere else. Throughout this section, you may see *The Wizarding World of Harry Potter* abbreviated to WWOHP.

The WWOHP opened at Universal Studios Hollywood in 2016. It followed the successful launch of Wizarding Worlds at Universal's parks in Florida and Japan.

Fun Fact: The attention to detail here is astounding. For example, in the restrooms at the Wizarding World, you can hear Moaning Myrtle.

Attractions

Flight of the Hippogriff

EX Yes	None	📷 No	⌄ 80 seconds	🔒 No	⏳ 20 to 30 minutes

A small rollercoaster where you soar on a Hippogriff and go past Hagrid's hut and motorcycle, as well as Buckbeak. Good family fun and a good starter coaster before putting your children on the likes of Revenge of the Mummy.

The ride reaches speeds of 40mph, so it does get reasonably fast.

Harry Potter and the Forbidden Journey

Yes	48"	📷 No	5 minutes	🔒 Yes	⏳ 60 to 120 minutes

A truly ground-breaking ride featuring projections, flexible ride vehicles and an incredibly detailed queue. This is the park's star attraction.

The opening of this attraction was a turning point in Universal Hollywood's history, catapulting its visitor numbers.

The queue line of this attraction is an attraction unto itself, as you wind your way through Hogwarts castle watching specially crafted scenes and experience moments like the famous trio in the Potter books and movies.

At the end of the queue, it is time for an incredible adventure - this is a simulator-style moving attraction that blurs the lines between physical sets and on-screen projections. Plus, the moment your enchanted bench first takes off is breathtaking.

Expect to encounter dementors, take part in a quidditch match, come face to face with dragons and much more.

There is a Single Rider queue line available, which can cut down wait times significantly; waits are usually about 50-75% shorter than the standard wait time in our experience, but this may vary.

Warning: We feel this ride creates mental strain due to the simulated sensations and the screens in front of you. This means that if you ride it more than once back-to-back, you may feel unwell.

Hidden Secret: When you are in Dumbledore's office hearing his speech, take a look at the books on the wall to the right of him. One of the books may do something very magical.

Interactive Wand Experiences

An interactive wand experience is available at the Wizarding World. To participate, guests must purchase an interactive wand from the Wizarding World's shops.

Interactive wands are priced at $49.95 (plus tax); these are a few dollars more than the non-interactive wands.

Once you have purchased a wand, look for the bronze medallions embedded in the streets that mark the various locations where you can cast spells. A map of the sites is included with each wand.

Once you are standing on a medallion, perform the correct spell. Simply draw the shape of the spell in the air with your wand and saying the name of the spell. Then, watch the magic come to life.

This is an enjoyable bit of extra entertainment, especially as the wands can be reused again and again during future visits.

Triwizard Spirit Rally

A six-minute dance contest between two competing wizard schools: men versus women.

The men's routine involves complex sword-fighting techniques, while the ladies dazzle with their ribbons and acrobatics.

It is a nice bit of entertainment and a great photo opportunity.

Frog Choir

A thirteen-minute series of songs inspired by the Harry Potter movies performed by Hogwarts students and their frogs, all done acapella with voices and no instruments.

There is an almost beat-box flair to this show, and it is a great piece of live entertainment.

Ollivanders

Length: 3 to 4 minutes
Express Pass Access: No
Average Wait: 30 to 60 mins

Technically, this is a pre-show to a shop. You enter Ollivanders in groups of about 25 people. One person in the group will be picked by the wandmaster to find the right wand for them.

Eventually, the right one is found, and they can choose to buy it when the group is moved to the shop area next door.

This is a fun experience that we highly recommend for Potter fans of all ages.

Character Meets and Drinks

To maintain the integrity of the Harry Potter areas, J.K. Rowling, the creator of the Harry Potter universe, specified that no branded drinks be sold in the Wizarding World – so, you will not find Coca Cola products here, for example.

You will only find Harry Potter branded drinks such as Butterbeer, water and some fruit squashes.

You are, of course, free to buy a drink elsewhere in the park, and bring it into the Wizarding World.

J.K. Rowling also prohibited character meets. So, you cannot meet Harry, Hermione, Hagrid, Draco, Ron or other characters from the films in the Wizarding World.

Restaurants

The restaurants in Hogsmeade are incredibly well-themed, and the Quick Service food here is some of the best in the park. We highly recommend you take a look inside the Hog's Head and Three Broomsticks, even if you do not plan on eating there.

• **Hog's Head Pub** – This pub is located in the same building as the Three Broomsticks. Serves alcoholic beer, a selection

of spirits, non-alcoholic Butterbeer and juices.

• **Three Broomsticks** – Serves breakfast meals. At lunch and dinner, you will find Cornish pasties, fish & chips, Shepherd's pie, smoked turkey legs, rotisserie smoked chicken and spareribs. Plus, desserts including Butterbeer potted cream. Entrees are $12-$25.

• **The Magic Neep and Ice Cream Cart** – This small cart

sells bottled drinks, beers, pre-packaged ice cream and fresh fruit.

Shops

The shops and merchandise in the Wizarding World are just as much of an experience as some of the rides. Be sure to step inside to admire the detail, and maybe even purchase a souvenir or two. Shops in the area include:

• **Filch's Emporium of Confiscated Goods** – Inside you will find themed apparel, mugs, photo frames and trinkets. It has almost everything a Harry Potter fan could ever want, and even sells Marauder's Maps.

• **Honeydukes** – For those with a sweet tooth, make sure to visit Honeydukes. You will find Bertie Bott's Every-Flavour Beans, chocolate frogs (with collectable trading cards), and tons of other candy.

• **Dervish & Banges** – The place to go for Hogwarts uniforms, as well as stationery and Quidditch items.

• **The Owl Post** – A real post office where you can send your letters or postcards to friends and family; these will get a Hogsmeade postmark and a Harry Potter stamp. You will also find stationery on sale here, as well as owl toys.

• **Gladrag's Wizard Wear** – Sells wizard apparel, including hats and accessories, as well as jewelry.

• **Hogwarts Express** – Train and Hogwarts Express themed merchandise, including Platform 9 3/4 branded items.

• **Ollivander's Wand Shop** – Purchase a unique Ollivander's wand, or choose from character replica wands.

• **Wizeacre's Wizarding Equipment** – Find all kinds of wizardry essentials here. From hourglasses to compasses, and telescopes to binoculars. Plus, themed apparel.

• **Zonko's Joke Shop** – This shop features all kinds of prank-filled items and toys, as well as novelty items and magic tricks, including Extendable Ears, Decoy Detonators and Fangled Flyers.

Note: Harry Potter branded wands are pricey; expect to pay $40 a piece for regular wands and $50 for interactive ones (plus tax).

Nighttime Shows

Universal hosts nighttime projection shows on Hogwarts Castle on select evenings throughout the year. At the moment two different shows have been shown:

• **The Nighttime Lights at Hogwarts Castle** – Celebrate the four Hogwarts houses as they are brought to life in a stunning spectacle of dazzling lights and music. Shown on select dates.

• **Dark Arts at Hogwarts Castle** – Feel the darker side of magic take hold. Prepare to face Dementors, Death Eaters and the Dark Lord, Voldemort in an ominous spectacle of light, music and live special effects. Shown on select dates.

Other shows may be proposed in the future. Shows take place throughout the night in the Wizarding World and feature music, projections and sometimes other special effects too.

Lower Lot

Once you have made it down the escalator (the 'StarWay') to the Lower Lot you will find more attractions, including some of the park's best.

Along the StarWay there are several viewing areas, so be sure to take in the views across the San Fernando Valley. You will be able to see other studios nearby including Warner Bros and Walt Disney Animation. Make sure to get some photos and use the plaques nearby to learn about what you can see from this unique viewpoint.

Attractions

TRANSFORMERS: The Ride-3D

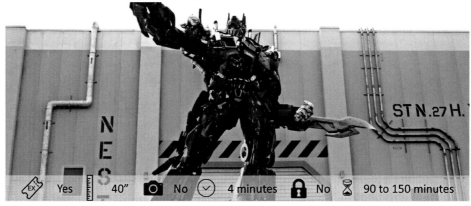

Yes	40"	No	4 minutes	No	90 to 150 minutes

TRANSFORMERS is a 3D screen-based moving dark ride. The storyline follows the Autobots (good guys) protecting the AllSpark from the Decepticons (bad guys).

Your ride vehicle moves from set to set, acting as a moving simulator immersing you in the action.

TRANSFORMERS: The Ride will be doubly impressive to fans of the movie franchise, though those who have not seen the movies will still enjoy the action-packed experience.

This ride often has one of the longest waits in the park outside of the Wizarding

World, so try to get here early in the day or towards the end, when crowds are at their lightest.

A Single Rider line is also available - we have found that it typically reduces your wait to about half of the regular standby line or less.

Dino Play

Height Restriction: 48 inches (1.20m) maximum
Express Pass Access: No

This play area themed to Jurassic Park contains dinosaur fossils and footprints for those not old enough to visit the mammoth water attraction next door. There are no water elements in the play area.

Revenge of The Mummy

A unique roller coaster featuring fire, smoke, forward and backwards motion, and more.

Revenge of The Mummy is one of the most fun coasters we have been on, starting as a slow-moving dark ride and then turning into a traditional roller coaster themed to the world of *The Mummy*.

Yes | 48" | Yes | 2 mins | Yes | 20 to 60 mins

Although the ride does not go upside-down and is not exactly the fastest attraction in California (though it does hit 45mph in less than 2 seconds), it does tell its story very well and immerses you in the atmosphere. It is a great thrill, with surprises throughout. The queue line is also incredibly detailed. If you have ridden the attraction with the same name at Universal Studios Florida, unfortunately, this is a pared down version that is just not as good.

This was due to the limited space available for construction. It is still, however, very enjoyable, and it is interesting to compare the similarities and differences.

A Single Rider line is offered.

Jurassic World: The Ride

Step into the world of Jurassic World on a riverboat, glide past huge dinosaurs, and enter through enormous doors just like in the movies.

However, this calm river adventure soon changes course.

Watch out for the T-Rex before you come splashing down an 84-foot drop! A Single Rider line is available.

Top Tip: You won't stay dry on this ride, but the driest seats are at the back.

Yes | 42" | No | 7 mins | No | 30 to 60 mins

Lockers are optional and paid.

This ride is closed until Summer 2019 for a major refurbishment.

DINING

Jurassic Café – Serves pizzas, burgers, roasted chicken, and salads, entrees are $12-$16.
Panda Express – Asian inspired food, including orange chicken & sushi, entrees are $14.
Starbucks Coffee – Serves Starbucks drinks, pastries and snacks, drinks are $4-$6.'
Studio Café – Serves wraps, hot dogs, sandwiches and salads, entrees are $7-$12.
Studios Scoop – Serves ice cream priced at $7-$10.

Universal Studios Hollywood Park Entertainment

Universal Studios Hollywood is home to live entertainment throughout the day. Character meets can be found throughout the park.

In addition to the live shows, such as *WaterWorld* listed in the park guide section, there are also a variety of character meet and greets on offer throughout Universal Studios Hollywood.

You will find characters in areas appropriate to them, for example, to meet Optimus Prime, head to near *Transformers: The Ride*. Many characters also meet in the Universal Plaza area.

Characters that you will often find throughout the park include:

• Optimus Prime, Bumbleebee and Megatron (from Transformers)
• The Minions, Gru & Margo (from Despicable Me)
• The Simpsons
• SpongeBob SquarePants – Near Universal Plaza
• Shrek, Princess Fiona, Puss in Boots and Donkey – In Upper Lot
• Curious George – Near Universal Studios Store
• Raptor Encounter – Includes a short show as the dinosaur is brought out and when it returns to its paddock at the end of meeting guests.
• Scooby-Doo and Shaggy – Universal Plaza
• Curious George – Near Cartooniversal
• Marilyn Monroe – By

Universal Studio Tour or near Universal Studios Store
• Woody and Winnie Woodpecker – Near Universal Studios Store

Other characters you may see include: Dora the Explorer, Dracula, Doc Brown, Beetlejuice, Frankenstein's Monster, and more.

Character times are printed on your park map and are also available live via the USH website at www.ushwaittimes.com. Other characters will also appear throughout the park without specific public schedules.

Unlike character meet

and greets at the nearby Disneyland Resort, character appearances at Universal Studios Hollywood do not usually require any planning or queueing. There may be a few people ahead of you to meet the characters, but we have never waited more than five minutes.

There are no parades at Universal Studios Hollywood.

You can also occasionally see celebrities being interviewed on 'EXTRA' hosted by Mario Lopez and co-hosts Tanika Ray and Renee Bargh. Interviews often take place at the Globe Fountain.

CityWalk

Universal's CityWalk is located just outside the theme park and within walking distance of several nearby hotels. There are stores, restaurants, a movie theater and other forms of entertainment.

CityWalk is free to all visitors, and no admission ticket is required. Parking is at the main Universal parking garages. CityWalk has ATMs, wheelchair rentals, lockers and a lost and found facility.

To get the latest CityWalk opening hours, and details on any live entertainment that may be taking place during your visit, check out www.citywalkhollywood.com. You can also call 818-622-4455 for additional information.

Shopping

If you fancy some shopping, there are plenty of places to visit, including:

Abercrombie & Fitch, Billabong, Bubba Gump Shrimp Store, The Dodgers Clubhouse, Fossil, Francesca's Collection, GUESS Accessories, Hard Rock Store, Hot Topic, IT'SUGAR, Locker Room (by Lids), The Los Angeles Sock Market, Nectar Bath Sweets, Shoe Palace, The Raider Image, Sephora, Sketchers, Sparky's, Things From Another World, Universal Studio Store and Zen Zone.

Dining

CityWalk is filled with unique dining experiences, as well as well-known chains. This section helps you choose where to eat on your next visit.

There are numerous Quick Service dining options:

Ben & Jerry's Ice Cream, Blaze Pizza, Cinnabon, The Crepe Café, Jamba Juice, KFC Express/Pizza Hut Express, Ludo Bird, Menchie's Frozen Yogurt, Mini Monster, Panda Express, Pink's Famous Hot Dogs, Popcornopolis, Smashburger, Starbucks Coffee, Subway, Taco Bell, Voodoo Doughnut and Wetzel's Pretzels

There are also many Table Service dining options at CityWalk:

Antojito's Cocina Mexicana (opens in 2019), Bubba Gump Shrimp Company, Buca di Beppo, Dongpo Kitchen, Hard Rock Café, Jimmy Buffet's Margaritaville, Johnny Rockets Burgers & Shakes, Karl Strauss Brewing Company, Samba Brazilian Steakhouse & Lounge, Tony Roma's, Wasabi and Vivo Italian Kitchen.

Reservations for Table Service establishments can be made at opentable.com or by calling restaurants directly.

Movie Theater

CityWalk features Universal Cinema, an AMC Theatre, including one screen that shows films in 7-story IMAX.

Tickets prices vary depending on the time of day and several other factors. A general ticket for an adult is priced at around $18. Child tickets are sold for kids ages 2 to 12 at $17. Senior tickets (over 60) and student ticket (13+ with a valid ID) discounts are also available. IMAX tickets cost up to $28.
Top Tip: If you watch a movie at the AMC movie theater at CityWalk, you get a rebate on your parking, reducing it to just $5. The discount is done at the movie theater box office.

iFly Indoor Skydiving

If you fancy an extra thrill, why not go for an indoor skydive? No experience is necessary, and the experience is available for ages 3 and up.

Pricing starts at $60 for two short flights, with many price points going up to over $400. Pictures and videos of your experience are available for an extra charge, though some packages include video footage.

If you're not flying, take a walk by anyway as the wind-chamber has a glass side so you can see all the action from the main walking paths at CityWalk.

CityWalk Nightlife

After dinner, some shopping or a skydive, you may want to opt to party the night away at one of three bars or nightclubs.

Howl at the Moon features live music, a dance party and huge drinks.

Samba Brazilian Steakhouse and Lounge provides delicious south-American fare and relaxed vibes in the lounge area. Enjoy happy hour from 3:00 p.m. to 7:00 p.m. daily, and live dancers.

The 5 Towers plaza is an outdoor concert venue in the center of CityWalk that regularly features live bands and other acts.

Out of state visitors, in particular, should be aware that the minimum drinking age in California is 21 and

anyone who appears to be aged under 30 will be asked for ID.

Somewhat surprisingly for many visitors, there is even a law-imposed curfew for under-18s. Under Los Angeles law it is unlawful "for any minor under the age of eighteen (18) years to be present in or upon any... public ground, public place or public building, place of amusement or eating place, vacant lot, or unsupervised place between the hours of 10:00 p.m. on any day and sunrise of the immediately following day".

This is waived if an adult accompanies them. CityWalk security is very much present in the evenings, and this law is strictly enforced.

Understanding the Parks

Universal Studios offers a variety of services designed to ease your day, from photo services to Express Passes, and Single Rider queue lines to package storage.

In-Park and Ride Photos

An in-park photographer often accompanies characters located around the park; sometimes these members of staff will also be present throughout the park by major landmarks too.

The photographers will happily use your cameras to take photos and will also take an "official" picture with their camera. You will be given a slip of paper with your photo number on it.

At any time until the end of the day, you can view all your in-park photos at the Photo Center in the entrance area of the park. On-ride photos function differently and can be purchased by the ride exit after having ridden the attraction. Rides that include on-ride photos are *The Simpsons Ride, Revenge of the Mummy,* and *Jurassic World: The Ride*.

Package storage

Universal Studios Hollywood's package storage service allows you to purchase any item in the park and have it stored until later in the day when you can pick it up. This means you won't have to carry it around all day.

You can choose to have your purchase sent to the Universal Studio Store, which is located near the exit. Purchases made throughout the day are sent here for you to pick up.

Mobile App

Universal Studios Hollywood's mobile app offers several features to enhance your visit, including:

• See live wait times for all rides and show schedules. You can even set alerts and be notified when the wait time for a specific ride drops to a time you specify.

• A park map to help you navigate your way around.

• Set a parking reminder to help find your car at the end of the day.

The app is available both on Apple and Android devices. Free XFinity Wi-Fi is available throughout the park, or you can connect using mobile data too.

Express Pass

If you are willing to pay to get on rides more quickly to reduce your wait, then Universal's Express Pass is perfect for you.

The Express Pass allows you to skip the regular queue lines at almost every attraction. You will be able to enter a separate queue line that is significantly shorter than the regular queue and drastically reduce your wait times.

For shows, you will be allowed entry before guests who do not have an Express Pass – usually 15 minutes before the show is due to begin. There will be a reserved seating area.

You may only use your faster access privileges once per participating attraction with the standard Express Pass or as many times as you want with the Express Unlimited option.

The Express Pass cannot be purchased as a standalone item; it is bundled with a theme park ticket for one all-inclusive price.

What does it cost?

Pricing varies according to how busy the theme park is. Tickets can be bought in advance online or at the theme park entrance. Remember the price of your Express pass includes admission, as well as your faster access privileges. The more expensive the Express ticket, the more useful it will be. An Express Pass with park admission costs between $179 and $279; the Unlimited version is an additional $30.

Which rides are not included?

Express Passes are valid on all attractions at the theme parks, except for Ollivanders. Triwizard Spirit Rally and the Frog Choir shows do not require advanced access, and you can walk into. Also, play areas such as Super Silly Fun Land do not have faster access as there are no queue lines to enter these.

How do I use it?

When at an attraction, look for the Express Pass entrance. This will usually be separate, but nearby, to the main queue line.

Here, show your Express Pass to the Team Member to enter the shorter dedicated queue line. Typically waits will be 10 minutes or less for rides even on the busiest days – often they will be much less.

As you are not in the main queue line, you may lose some of the storyline told in the queue. Each member of your party will need their own Express Pass.

Do I need an Express Pass?

If you are prepared to get to the theme park before it opens, it is achievable to see all shows and do all the rides in the park without an Express pass during regular park operating hours.

If, however, you plan to visit during a busy period (e.g. Christmas, Spring Break, Summer) or if you cannot be at the park entrance just before opening time, an Express Pass may be worth the extra cost for a hassle-free visit with no waits.

VIP Tour Experience

The VIP Experience is a step up from the Express Pass and the ultimate way to experience Universal Studios Hollywood, including several experiences that are unique to this tour.

This is a full-day service beginning from before you even step foot in the park, with valet parking and park admission included. There is even a dedicated theme park entrance. Once inside the park, you can enjoy a continental breakfast in the private VIP lounge.

Throughout the day, you will be escorted to the Express Pass entrance at Universal's most popular shows and attractions, and have lunch in the private VIP dining room.

After your tour, you get unlimited Express Pass access to all the rides on your own. You will be in a small group with other people who have also purchased the VIP experience.

Movie fans will love the private Studio Tour, with a small tram just for your group. You can even step off the tram and roam some of the sets, enter soundstages, tour the audio department, and enter the movie studio's largest prop warehouse.

Pricing starts at $359 per person and goes up to $419 depending on the date; children under five years old may not take part in this experience.

In addition, if you would like to reserve a VIP tour just for your family or group, this can be arranged with a private VIP tour.

Is the VIP Experience worth it?

Movie fans with spare cash will love this tour, especially with all the extra exclusive backstage experiences. If you are not interested in the additional features of the studio tour, you may be best off with a standard Express pass. If money is no object, this is hands down the best way to experience the park and the best premium studio experience in Hollywood.

Stroller and Wheelchair Rentals

Universal Studios Hollywood offers stroller, wheelchair and motorized ECV rentals. The rental area is located to the right-hand side after the theme park turnstiles.

You can rent the following:

* Single Stroller – $15
* Double Stroller – $25
* Wheelchairs – $15, plus a $25 deposit.
* ECVs – $60, plus a $25 deposit.

ECVs must be operated by a single person aged 18 years old or over. Wheelchairs can also be rented at CityWalk. Strollers must be folded before using the StarWay between Upper and Lower lots.

Internet Access

You can find free Wi-Fi access throughout the theme park; the network is called "UNIVERSAL" or "xfinitywifi". The theme park also has a handy mobile website (www.ushwaittimes.com), as well as an app, that allows you to see attraction wait times in real time, as well as show and character schedules.

Ride Lockers

Two of the rides at USH – Harry Potter and the Forbidden Journey and Revenge of the Mummy – do not allow you to take your belongings onto them; loose articles must be placed in free lockers. Here is how they work:

• Approach a locker station located by the entrance to these rides;
• Select 'Rent a locker' from the touch screen;
• Put your fingerprint on the reader, and you will be assigned a locker;
• Go to the locker, put your belongings inside and press the green button next to the locker to lock the door. It is vital that you do this to make sure the locker is actually locked! If you forget to press the green button, the locker will automatically lock 5 seconds after the door is closed.

The lockers are free for a certain period. This is always longer than the current posted attraction wait time. For example, a 90-minute wait for Forbidden Journey would typically allow you 120 or 150 minutes of locker rental time to allow you to wait in the queue line, experience the ride and collect your belongings with plenty of time to spare.

If you keep your belongings in the lockers longer than the free period, charges apply.

As well as the free lockers, larger paid-for ride lockers are also available to rent. For most people, though, these won't be necessary.

Lockers for Jurassic Park: The Ride are optional and not free.

Top Tip 1: If you rent a locker and your free time has expired because the wait time was longer than expected, tell a Team Member who will sort out the issue.

Top Tip 2: If you forget your locker number, there is a feature on the locker terminals that will help you find it.

Top Tip 3: Lockers for water rides are not free. In this case, you could simply walk to a locker for another ride where they are free. This can save you a decent amount of money throughout a trip. *Revenge of the Mummy* has lockers and is close enough to *Jurassic World: The Ride* and often has long locker rental times, for example.

Top Tip 4: The touchscreens on the lockers are unresponsive, meaning that it can be hard for the touchscreen to register your finger touches. We recommend using your fingernails to touch the screen to solve this problem.

All-day park locker rentals: The entry plaza locates non-ride specific lockers – the cost varies depending on the size of locker required:

Locker sizes are as follows:
• $8 Lockers: Height – 12¾", Width – 11" and Length – 16½"
• $12 Lockers: Height – 16", Width – 8" and Length – 16"
• $15 Lockers: Height – 21½", Width – 11" and Length – 16"

The lockers accept both cash and credit/debit cards. Guests may access these all-day lockers as many times as they want throughout the day.

Child Switch

When two adults visit Universal Studios Hollywood with a child who does not or cannot ride certain attractions, there can be a problem if the adults want to ride a thrill ride – each adult would need to queue separately while the other waits with the child. They would then swap. This would mean that they would wait twice for each attraction. However, at USH the solution is Child Switch.

Simply go to a Team Member at a participating attraction entrance and ask to use Child Switch. Each ride works a little differently, but generally, one adult will go into the standard queue line while another adult is directed to a child swap waiting area.

Once the first adult has queued up and ridden the attraction, they proceed to the Child Switch area. Here the first adult will stay with the child, and the person who originally sat with the child gets to ride straight away, without having to wait in the queue line again.

This procedure may vary from attraction to attraction – make sure you ask the Universal Team Member at each attraction entrance about the process.

Child Switch is available at *Harry Potter and the Forbidden Journey, Despicable Me: Minion Mayhem, Revenge of the Mummy, Jurassic World: The Ride, Transformers: The Ride – 3D,* and *The Simpsons Ride.*

Ride Height Requirements

Many attractions at Universal Studios Hollywood have height requirements meaning that not everyone in your party may be able to enjoy every attraction. Height requirements are put in place for the safety of all guests to ensure they fit in the ride vehicles correctly. You will need to be measured at the entrance to each ride by a ride operator if you are close to the height limit – their word is final.

This section helpfully lists all attractions (except those without height requirements) in ascending order of height.

• Flight of the Hippogriff – 39 inches (0.99m)
• Despicable Me: Minion Mayhem – 40 inches (1.02m)
• TRANSFORMERS: The Ride-3D – 40 inches (1.02m)
• The Simpsons Ride – 40 inches (1.02m)
• Jurassic World: The Ride – 42 inches (1.07m)
• Revenge of the Mummy – 48 inches (1.22m)
• Harry Potter and the Forbidden Journey – 48 inches (1.22m)

Single Rider

One of the best ways to significantly reduce your waiting time is to use Single Rider lines. This is an entirely separate queue used to fill free spaces on ride vehicles. For example, if a ride vehicle can seat 8 people and a group of 4 boards, followed by a group of 3, then a 'Single Rider' will fill the space.

Single Rider queues make wait times shorter for everyone as all spaces on ride vehicles are filled.

Single Riders typically board more quickly, and the regular queue moves quicker as all the single riders are not in it!

If the parks are extremely busy then Single Rider lines may be closed. This happens when the wait in the Single Rider line is greater than the regular line. If the Single Rider queue line is full and cannot accommodate more guests, it will also be temporarily closed. If the park is almost empty, sometimes these lines do not operate either.

If you are travelling as part of a group, you can still use the Single Rider queue line – be aware that you will ride separately, but you can always meet each other at the exit after the ride.

Single Rider lines are available on *Harry Potter and the Forbidden Journey, Jurassic World: The Ride, Transformers: The Ride,* and *Revenge of the Mummy.*

Guests with Disabilities

Visiting a theme park can be a complicated process for someone with a disability, but Universal Studios Hollywood has worked hard to give people in this situation as much of the full theme park experience as possible. Although we could not possibly cover every kind of disability in this section, we have tried to include as much information as possible.

Universal Guest Assistance Pass

A Universal Guest Assistance Pass can ease the day for visitors. To obtain one you will need to visit Guest Services (to the right after the turnstiles) and ask for the Guest Assistance Pass.

Although it is not required, we strongly recommend you get a note from your doctor (in English) explaining what exactly you need help with - whether it is not waiting in the sun or not waiting for prolonged periods standing up or not waiting in crowded areas. It all depends on your situation. Your doctor does NOT need to explain your disability, just what help you require.

The Universal Team Members at Guest Services will ask you questions to determine eligibility and what type of help you need. As mentioned, a letter from a doctor is not required but will greatly assist this process. You will be issued a Guest Assistance Pass, and it will be explained.

Using the Pass:
When you reach an attraction you wish to ride, show your Guest Assistance Pass to the Team Member at the ride entrance (the 'greeter'). If the regular attraction wait time is less than 30 minutes, you will be immediately directed to an alternate queue.

If the regular wait time for the attraction is 30 minutes or longer, then the greeter will write down a time on your Pass to return – we will call this a 'reservation' in this guide.

The time of this reservation will be the current time, plus the attraction queue length, Eg. It is 1:00 pm and there is a 35-minute wait, so your return time will be for 1:35 pm.

When that time comes around, show your pass with the reservation time at the ride entrance and you will be allowed entry through the alternative queue. This is NOT a front-of-the-line ticket and waits can still be up to 15 minutes.

You can only hold one 'reservation' at a time, though you may enjoy faster entry to rides with less than a 30-minute wait, even if you have an existing reservation.

If you want to change the attraction you have a reservation for, go to the next attraction and make a reservation with the attraction's greeter at the entrance. This will void your previous reservation.

Other Assistance for Disabled Guests

Deaf/Hard of Hearing
– For guests who are deaf or hard of hearing, many in-park shows have signed performances. These can be reserved at no charge with at least one week's notice by contacting Guest Relations at 1-800-UNIVERSAL or e-mailing guest.communications@ nbcuni.com.

Assistive listening devices for guests with hearing impairments are provided at Guest Relations free of charge. Amplified handsets are at all phone locations.

Mobility Impairment and Wheelchairs – Universal Studios Hollywood has been designed to be as wheelchair-accessible as possible. All the shopping and dining facilities are accessible. Guests who would like to use a stroller as a wheelchair should ask for a special tag from Guest Relations.

Stage shows also have designated areas for wheelchair users and their parties. Most rides are accessible – some will require a transfer; others will allow you to ride in your

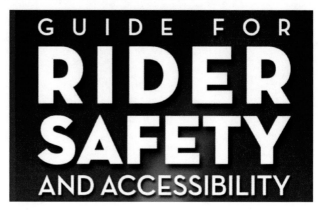

wheelchair. Guests must transfer to a wheelchair in queues.

Note that you do not NEED to have a Guest Assistance Pass if you are in a wheelchair as all rides have an accessible entrance, but it can make things easier when there are particularly long waits, so we do recommend it.

If you, or someone you are with, have a disability that is not easily seen we thoroughly recommend the use of the Guests Assistance Passes – without one you will need to use the regular queue line.

Service Animals are permitted throughout the

theme parks, but each attraction will have a specific way of boarding. The greeters at the entrance of each attraction will be able to provide more information.

Rides and shows:
Special restrictions apply to guests with prosthetic limbs and guests with oxygen tanks. More information about rides and shows specifically is available through the Riders Guide for Rider Safety & Accessibility Guide (PDF file). It can be downloaded from www.bit.ly/hollydisab. Printed copies are also available at Guest Services.

Dining

When visiting Universal Studios Hollywood, you will find an abundance of food choices, from standard theme park fare to Table Service dining, as well as snack carts.

Theme park fast food is generally priced at about twice what you would pay outside the parks. A $5 hamburger becomes $10-$12, and a drink will be about $4. A full quick service meal will cost you between $14 and $24 depending on what options you choose.

Dining Reservations

In the theme parks, there are no Table Service dining locations, but only Quick Service eateries.

Table Service locations are available just outside the theme park gates in CityWalk. As such, there are no reservations for any in-park restaurants. If you wish to make reservations

for CityWalk, most locations can be book at OpenTable.com. Otherwise, you should call the restaurants directly as each is operated independently, and there is no centralized booking system.

Except for peak dates, you should be able to get a reservation for most

restaurants a week or so in advance. If there is a specific place you want to eat, we recommend you book your table as early as possible. However, we have frequently decided that we would like to eat a particular location and have known to get reservations on the very same day.

Top Table Service Restaurants

Universal has several Table Service restaurants in CityWalk. We have rounded up those that you really should not miss out on below. Note that prices and menus change all the time with seasons and chefs – those that we have listed were correct as of when we ate at the locations and act only as examples.

1. Samba Brazilian Steakhouse & Lounge – Gourmet Brazilian cuisine done at its best, served family-style on skewers. There are even all-you-can-eat options for those wanting to fill up ($25 at lunch and $60 at dinner). The cocktails are excellent.

2. Buca di Beppo – Top quality Italian food, served in huge portions and with friendly service. Dishes are served family-style to share meaning that prices are reasonable per person. Large pasta dishes for 3 to 5 people are typically about $39, for example. There is a

good wine selection too.

3. Tony Roma's – Yes, Tony's is a chain, but it can't be missed for the best baby back ribs. The steaks here are equally delicious, and there are many other dishes available. Portions are generous.

Top Quick Service Restaurants

Sometimes you may not want to sit down and have a three-course meal. You might want to use that time to watch a show, walk around the parks or ride your favorite attraction again – but that does not mean you want to compromise on taste.

Here are our favorite on-site Quick Service restaurants. Note that prices and entrees change often; those listed were correct as of the last time we ate at the locations and should be taken as examples.

1. Three Broomsticks – Everything about this restaurant puts it top of the pile of quick service locations: the atmosphere, the food and its opening hours. Three Broomsticks is open for all three meals: breakfast, lunch and dinner, and is the only restaurant inside The Wizarding World of Harry Potter.

Entrees are priced between $9 and $25. Breakfast entree choices include breakfasts from around the world. Lunch and dinner fare revolves around British dishes with some American classics available too. You will find fish & chips, shepherd's pie, as well as smoked turkey legs, rotisserie smoked chicken and spareribs.

2. Krusty Burger – If you want the slimiest of burgers, then this is the place to go. Designed to be exactly as "artery-clogging" as the burgers are in 'The Simpsons' cartoons, Krusty Burger will not win any awards for being exotic or healthy, but this location has hands down the best-tasting burgers at Universal.

Entrees are priced between $13 and $15 with fries included. As well as burgers, you will find barbecue rib sandwiches and hot dogs. The burgers are, however, an acquired taste – many guests report they did not like the taste of the meat.

3. Gru's Lab Café – Themed around Despicable Me, there is a variety of choice here making it a good place to go for all tastes. From pulled pork sandwiches to tasty rotisserie chicken, every entrée we have had here has been a solid choice.

For those looking for some Asian cuisine, try Dr Nefario's Lab Salad. Plus, try the desserts to round off your meal. They are incredible! Entrees are priced between $12 and $16.

4. Jurassic Café – This is the best place to eat on the Lower Lot, in our opinion, serving mainly American favorites. The selection includes fresh salads, turkey legs, roasted chicken, personal pizzas and gourmet burgers. It is not hugely adventurous, but there is a good chance you will find something here for most people, especially kids. Entrees are $12 to $16.

5. Cocina Mexicana – Lastly, this location gets a mention for those looking for Mexican cuisine. You will find burritos, tacos and salads. Entrees are priced at $13 to $14.

Tips, Savings and More

This section covers various ways to make your trip better - from ways to save time and money, to Early Park Admission.

Money Saving Tips

Take food in with you
Universal allows you to bring your own food into the park. Whether it is a bag of chocolates or a drink, you can purchase these items at a fraction of the price anywhere outside of Universal property.

For drinks, why not put them in a cooling bag (hard-sided coolers are not allowed in the parks), or freeze them to drink throughout the day. Food should be fine in a backpack throughout the day.

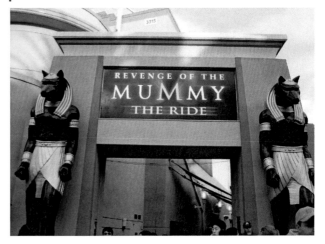

Glass containers and bottles are not permitted.

Buy tickets in advance
Do not buy tickets at the gate – you will waste time and pay more than you need to.

As you are reading this guide, we can safely assume that you are planning to go, so there is no excuse not to buy your tickets in advance. You can do this over the phone, online at universalstudios hollywood.com or through a third party. You will save $10 per ticket by pre-purchasing them.

You do not NEED Express Pass
By following our Touring Plan, you will be able to see the entirety of the theme park in just one day. If you do not wish to wait in queue lines, however, then Express Passes are necessary.

Stay off-site
If you are on a budget, then stay off-site. There are many hotels just off Universal Studios Hollywood property – a two to three-minute drive away, or a 15-minute walk. Or with the convenient Metro subway system, you can get a hotel room slightly further away for a better price.

These rooms can cost a fraction of the price of the on-site hotels.

Character photos
When getting your picture taken with a character, ask the photographer to take one with your camera

too. This way you get free images instead of paying the park's exorbitant prices.

Free lockers
Universal charges for lockers on Jurassic World: The Ride as this is a water ride but not on any other rides. Simply, walk to a non-water ride and use those lockers.

If you are doing this, be prepared to do some extra walking to save a few dollars. Also, be ready to look around for the ride with the longest wait times to store your belongings.

Harry Potter and the Forbidden Journey often has lockers with long access times, but *Revenge of the Mummy* is much closer to *Jurassic World: The Ride*.

Operating Hours and Ride Closures

Universal Studios Hollywood is open 365 days a year, and operating hours of the theme park vary according to demand. On days when it is expected that there will be a surge in visitors, the parks are open longer, and when there aren't so many people, the park closes earlier.

We strongly advise that you check opening hours before your visit. They may change closer to the date of your visit, so do re-check.

Park operating hours can be verified several months in advance at www.universalstudioshollywood.com/calendar-and-hours/.

Ride refurbishments also happen throughout the year to keep rides operating safely and efficiently.

As Universal is open 365 days a year, it does not close to refurbish rides like some other theme parks. Therefore, rides

and attractions must close throughout the year to be renewed. Refurbishments tend to avoid the busier times of the year. For example, *Jurassic World: The Ride* is often closed during the winter months (Jan to Mar). The refurbishment schedule is posted online.

As well as planned refurbishments, rides may close for technical issues or weather-related reasons.

How to Spend Less Time Waiting In Line

Park opening
Get to the theme park well before it officially opens - ideally, 30 minutes before opening. Remember it will take time to park your car and walk to the theme park. The park often opens earlier than advertised, particularly during busy periods.

Early morning is the least busy time - in the first hour you can usually do 3 or 4 of the biggest rides - this takes several hours during the rest of the day.

Use Single Rider lines

If you do not mind riding separately from the rest of your party, use the Single Rider queue lines. They reduce your wait time significantly and are available at several major attractions.

Touring Plans
We have included a carefully designed Touring Plan to tell you what order to do the attractions in - follow this.

The 59-minute rule
The time that Universal announces as closing its parks is when the queue lines (not the rides) close.

Anyone in the queue line at park closing time will ride, no matter how long the wait is. If you have one final ride to do and it is getting to park closing time, get in the queue quickly to ride.

This rule may not apply if an attraction has an exceptionally long wait time that would cause it to keep running for a long time after the park closing time.

Top Tip: The last Studio Tour leaves well before the park closes (usually 1 hour 40 minutes before).

Early Park Admission

Benefit from much shorter waits at select attractions with Early Park Admission (EPA).

During most of the year, Universal Studios Hollywood offers 30 minutes of early entry to *The Wizarding World of Harry Potter,* and all its shops, restaurants and

attractions.

This benefit is available to guests who purchase park tickets directly on the USH website at www.universalstudios hollywood.com and also for guests who purchase a Universal Vacation Package including park tickets and a Preferred Hotel.

As *The Wizarding World of Harry Potter* is the most popular part of the park, accessing it early in the day ensures lower wait times – a valuable benefit.

Entry is 30 minutes before regular park opening. During low season, this benefit may be unavailable.

Comparing Universal Studios Hollywood & Disneyland Resort

Universal Studios Hollywood cannot be studied in a vacuum as it is not the only theme park in the L.A. area. Far from it; if it were not for the other big competitor in the district, Universal most likely would not even have built a theme park in California. We are, of course referring to the Disneyland Resort: home to the first real theme park – and the second most visited theme park resort in the world.

The two resorts have many similarities and many differences, so if you have visited one and not the other, this section should be able to provide you with an insight into what to expect. We hope this will help you be more prepared for your Universal Studios Hollywood experience.

Resort Size

Universal Studios Hollywood, including CityWalk, the theme park and the entire studio filming area measures in at roughly 350 acres. However, if you exclude the Studio Tour, the actual theme park is a mere 40 acres in size.

In comparison, the Disneyland Resort measures in at about 440 acres. Disneyland Park is 84 acres in size (double the size of Universal Studios) and a second theme park, Disney's California Adventure, measures in at 67 acres.

The Disneyland Resort, therefore, boasts two theme parks, three on-site hotels and a shopping and entertainment district, Downtown Disney. Universal Studios Hollywood has one theme park (albeit with a vast Studio Tour), CityWalk for shopping and entertainment, and a few nearby hotels not managed by Universal.

Character meet and greets

At the Disneyland Resort, you have to plan which characters you want to meet and when, and even have the possibility of making Fastpass reservations.

At Universal Studios Hollywood, meeting characters is more spontaneous, and you should never have to wait more than 5 or 10 minutes to meet a character. Compare that to a 45-minute wait for the princesses at Disney, and you can see the difference.

Nightlife

As far as nightlife is concerned, Universal has a more adult feel than Disney. Universal has full-blown bars and clubs such as Howl at the Moon, whereas Disney does not have anything comparable.

You will see many more families out at Disney, compared to Universal however and, generally speaking, Disney caters better for family-friendly activities than purely for adults.

Planning and Off-Season

A vacation to Disneyland requires more planning as it is a multi-day destination. You will need to decide between one-park or two-park tickets, the length of stay and you need a strategy to make the most out of your visit and avoid huge queue lines.

You need to understand the Fastpass system to reduce your time waiting in queue lines, get to shows well in advance and know which rides to visit when. Plus, you should plan for fireworks and parades and how you will integrate these into your day. There are over 80 attractions to choose from, so chances are you will have to pick and choose between them, and you will not experience them all.

Universal Studios Hollywood's significant advantage is the fact it is so small. There is only one theme park, there are only a small number of attractions and therefore planning is much simpler. There is no need to reserve a restaurant in the park, as no in-park restaurants take reservations, there is no equivalent of a Fastpass system (you have either bought an Express Pass or you haven't), ticketing options are more straightforward, and shows and rides are easier to get to. You should have a strategy for the rides (see our Touring Plan for a perfect example of this), but as there are fewer than 15 attractions, you can do them all in one day with a bit of planning.

Visiting the theme parks during school breaks means that they are going to be busy; the kids are out of school and parents want children to have fun, so the theme parks are naturally going to be filled with guests. What about out of season? Such as September during school time, or February.

At the Disneyland Resort, you can expect to find crowds year round. There are quieter days than others, but there is never going to be a day at the Disneyland Resort that you can stroll onto *Radiator Springs Racers* within 5 minutes; it simply does not happen. Disneyland also has a considerable number of annual Passholders who visit very frequently; the resort even had to suspend sales of certain passes in 2014 as crowds were becoming detracting from the guest experience.

This is different at Universal; there are still lots of times of the year in the off-season when almost every ride is a walk-on – these are times when you can

experience *Harry Potter and the Forbidden Journey* in a matter of minutes instead of waiting an hour or two! The off-season still exists at Universal. This has a lot to do with the target demographic of Universal with older teens likely being in school longer and young adults working, whereas very young kids can visit Disney year-round. Annual Passholders at Universal are also likely to visit less often as there are fewer things to do.

To compare, Universal Studios Hollywood had just over 9 million visitors in 2018. The Disneyland Resort in comparison saw just under 10 million visitors at Disney's California Adventure, but over 18.5 million at Disneyland Park.

Having said this, if Universal continues to grow in popularity as it has done in recent years, it is possible that the same 'lack of off-season' situation will develop, particularly as the park has a minimal number of attractions.

Hotel accommodation

Universal Studios Hollywood does not run any hotels itself, but there are two nearby on-site hotels run by major hotel chains. It is a short walk from both of these to the park, or a shuttle bus is available. There is no extra Universal theming to these hotels, and you only get Early Park Admission if you book with Universal Vacations.

The hotels and the theme park at USH are very much two separate entities, and the staff at the hotel are not hugely knowledgeable as to the theme parks. Many hotels are available in the surrounding area.

In contrast, the Disneyland Resort has three on-site hotels owned and operated by Disneyland. These offer extra benefits such as package delivery, Extra Magic Hours (Early Park Admission), a food credit scheme, the ability to charge purchases in the theme park to your room key, and staff who are knowledgeable about the parks.

There is no need for shuttle buses from the on-site Disney hotels as they are all within walking distance. Disney's Grand Californian Hotel offers exceptional theming and even a private entrance to one of the

theme parks. These are just some of the advantages of everything being run by the same company.

In addition, there are hundreds of non-official and partner hotel options just as close to Disneyland as some of the official hotels.

Attractions, lockers and theming

Disney is known for the nostalgia of its rides, with some having stuck around since opening day, over 60 years ago.

You can still ride classics such as Peter Pan's Flight, though advancements have been made as Walt Disney always wanted his park to "never be complete" and to "keep moving forward". You can now meet the newest Marvel superheroes, hop on a flight around the world in *Soarin'* and get some high-speed thrills at *Radiator Springs Racers*. Disney appeals to everyone of every age, but with a stronger focus on family adventures. The theming at Disney's parks is second to

none, with environments that immerse you in every direction you look. The construction of a Star Wars land will only add to this.

In contrast, Universal Studios Hollywood is seen as more of an adult park. A good number of the attractions have minimum height limits, there are just two small play areas for kids, and many of Universal's rides are reasonably intense and generally more thrilling than at Disney.

Whereas at Disneyland you can take your belongings onto every single ride and keep them at your feet or in your pockets, at Universal

Studios Hollywood, you must leave them in (free) lockers while you are riding a few of the attractions.

This can be annoying, but admittedly, it does seem safer for guests.

Theming in the Universal parks is sparse and, despite the effort to theme specific areas, it does feel odd how things change from one corner to the next. The *Wizarding World of Harry Potter* is one of the best-themed environments in any theme park, but the visual intrusions from the park's other areas do ruin it a bit.

Dining

The food at Universal Studios Hollywood is generally slightly cheaper than at the Disneyland Resort.

However, there is nowhere near as much variety at Universal as there is at Disney; you will pretty much have to stick to standard theme park food at USH. The most significant difference in our opinion is the quality and taste; while food at Disney's parks is not gourmet by any standard, in general, it is better than Universal's.

There are also no Table Service restaurants inside the theme park at Universal, and the choice at CityWalk is limited. At Disneyland, character and Table Service meals are a big part of the experience, and the choice is much larger.

Fastpass versus Express Pass

At the Disneyland Resort, your park ticket enables you to make free Fastpass reservations, which let you skip the regular queue lines by reserving a time to ride. These are made by visiting Fastpass machines by each attraction you wish to ride, inserting your park ticket into the machine and getting your Fastpass ticket. Your Fastpass ticket will give you a 1-hour time slot to return, and you can usually only hold one Fastpass reservation at a time. It is a bit of a complicated system to understand, but guidebooks (like our very own *The Independent Guide to Disneyland*) go through the whole process. The system only works on a select number of major attractions at the park.

The Express Pass at Universal allows you near-instant entry to every major attraction for a fee. This fee is in addition to your admission ticket and usually adds on at least $100 per person. You can only use your Express Pass privileges once per attraction.

Leaving aside the fact that

Disney's FastPass is better value as it is free, Universal's Express Pass (because of its paid nature) works better: there is rarely more than a 10-minute wait, you do not make reservations in advance, it is simple to understand, fewer people use it and it is available for every single attraction. It is simple to use and useful.

Special Events

Both Universal and Disney know that to keep people visiting all year-round, they need to offer seasonal events.

For Halloween, Universal offers a horror-filled portrayal of the season with Halloween Horror Nights,

whereas Disney goes for a "not so scary" approach. Both resorts host after-hours paid events.

Christmas, however, is a *much* bigger deal at Disney, with limited time shows, decorations, lighting ceremonies, nighttime

spectaculars and more. Two attractions, *Haunted Mansion* and *"it's a small world"*, even completely re-theme their interiors for this season. Universal holds its own Christmas event season inspired by The Grinch with decorations, shows and character meets.

Seasonal Events

Universal Studios Hollywood offers several seasonal events towards the end of the year. Whether it be horror mazes or Holiday cheer, the Universal team have it covered. This section covers the two main seasonal events each year.

Halloween Horror Nights

Mid-September to Early November

Halloween Horror Nights is an evening extravaganza where there are heavily themed haunted houses, live entertainment and scare zones where "scareactors" roam around to frighten you. The theming is incredible at this event and unlike any other scare attraction. You will also find most of the attractions open inside the park.

At the time of writing very little detail has been announced for 2019. Information on the 2019 event should be released between July and the end of August 2019.

Halloween Horror Nights (HHN) is very popular and Universal Studios Hollywood does get extremely crowded during these events. Expect waits of 90 minutes or longer for each haunted house on most nights. This is one time when we highly recommend purchasing the HHN Express Pass if you want the full experience and to see everything, though it is an additional supplement that doubles the price of admission. You may need to make multiple visits to see everything on offer.

Dates:
Halloween Horror Nights runs on select nights from 7:00 pm to 2:00 am. Dates

for 2019 have not yet been announced but we do know that the event will start on Friday, September 13th and usually runs until early November. The further your dates are from Halloween, the less crowded your visit is likely to be.

What is part of HHN?
Each year, the entertainment changes at Halloween Horror Nights, which keeps people coming back. For reference, in 2018, there were eight different haunted houses/ mazes. Guests can expect the haunted houses to last about 3 to 5 minutes each. The line-up for 2019 includes Frankenstein Meets the Wolf Man, Holidayz in Hell and Stranger Things.

There were also five scare zones in 2018, where characters roam the zones causing fear; here you do not need to queue to be

scared. We expect 2019 to be similar. Also, scattered around the park are scare- actors with chainsaws... ready to run at you.

As far as live shows, 2018 offered a show by San Diego-based dance troupe Jabbawockees.

Finally, one of the highlights of the event every year is the Terror Tram – exclusive to this park. It is a short tram ride, followed by a walkthrough horror maze experience. In 2018, it was called 'Hollywood Harry's Dreadtime Stories'.

Select attractions are also open during HHN. In 2018 these were: *Transformers, Revenge of the Mummy,* and *The Simpsons Ride.* Queues for attractions are generally non-existent, as the focus is on the scares for most people. Guests with an Express Pass can use it for both the mazes and rides.

Universal warns the event "may be too intense for young children and is not recommended for children under the age of 13". No costumes or masks are allowed at the event.

Is The Wizarding World of Harry Potter part of HHN?
In previous years, this part of the park has not opened for HHN. We expect the *Wizard World* to be closed in 2019 as with past years.

Pricing:
Ticket sales for 2019 were not yet open at the time of writing. For reference, in 2018 a single general admission ticket was priced at $75 to $104 on the gate. Discounts of up to $30 are available at www. halloweenhorrornights. com/halloween in advance. We recommend you get

your tickets in advance to save money; tickets sell out for popular dates.

You can also add a night of Halloween Horror Nights to your daytime park ticket. In 2018, this was priced between $199 and $269.

An after-2pm ticket is also available with access to the theme park from 2 pm, plus HHN access. Multi-night tickets also start from $169.

HHN Express Passes:
Express Passes are available that combine a Halloween Horror Nights entry ticket plus expedited entry into each horror maze and attraction once, as well as reserved seating at shows. Pricing ranges from $17-$229. Express Passes may sell out in advance.

RIP Experience:
The $329-$399 RIP

Experience includes VIP entry, unlimited front of the line access to all rides and mazes, valet parking, and access to the private VIP lounge with music and food.

HHN Top Tips:
• Although the event is listed as starting at 7:00 pm, you can get early access to the park from 5:45 pm to 6:15 pm, with select mazes opening from 6:30 pm.
• Costumes and masks are not allowed, and you will be refused entry into the park. No food and drink may be brought from outside either. Security is very tight.
• The least busy days of the week are generally Thursdays and Sundays. Take a look at the pricing online: the cheaper it is, the less busy it is likely to be.
• Terror Tram closes before the rest of the park. See the park schedule.

Christmas

December

The Grinchmas celebration is included as part of your daytime admission and is not an extra charged event like HHN

Dates are announced only 2 to 3 weeks before the event; the event runs on select dates only.

As part of Grinchmas, you can expect:

• A tree-lighting show
• Meet and greet with The Grinch, Max (Grinch's dog) and the Whoville Characters
• Martha May & The Who Dolls Dance Performance
• The Who-liday Singers Acapella Performance
• The Whoville Post Office to write postcards
• Exclusive Grinchmas themed food on sale

As this is not your traditional Christmas season, there are no meets with Santa Claus at the park.

Christmas at the Wizarding World of Harry Potter runs daily in December with a seasonal projection show at night, Christmas decorations, themed songs from the Frog Choir, and even snow.

New Year's Eve

31st December

For the transition into the New Year, head to USH - the park opens early at 8:00 am and stays open until 2:00 am

on 1st January (rides close at 1:00 am). You can expect live DJs, fireworks displays, specialty food and drink and

more entertainment.

The event is included with regular park admission.

The Definitive Touring Plan

To make the most of your time at Universal Studios Hollywood, we highly recommend you follow this touring plan.

Using this Plan

This touring plan is not designed in order for you to have a leisurely, slow day through the park, it is designed to get as much accomplished as possible, while still having fun.

This may mean crossing the park back and forth in order to save you from waiting in long queue lines, but ultimately it means you can get the most out of your Universal experience.

Our touring plan will have you riding the most popular attractions (those with the longest waits) at the start and end of the day when they are least busy; during the middle of the day you will be visiting the attractions that have consistent wait times, and watching shows. This enables you to maximize your time.

Attractions are generally busiest between 11:00am and 4:00pm. Before 11:00am, people are still making their way to the park; after 4:00pm, most people have seen enough for the day. If the parks are open until late, you will find that most rides are 'walk-ons' in the last hour of park operation.

This touring plan presumes you do not have an Express Pass. If you do, then you can explore the park in whatever order you want, as you won't have to worry about waiting in the queue lines.

At the moment, Universal Studios Hollywood does not have an abundance of attractions meaning that wait times can be long throughout the park. It is, however, perfectly possible to do all the rides in the park on the same day with some planning.

The key to this touring plan is to arrive at the park well before it opens; that means being at the parking garages at least 60 minutes before park opening if you are driving in, which is when the parking garages open.

If you want to buy tickets on the day, you will need to be at the park gates at least 45 minutes before opening.

Otherwise, be at the park gates at least 30 minutes before opening with your park admission in hand. Park gates regularly open up to 30 minutes before the official stated opening time.

Using this touring plan: If there is a particular attraction you do not wish to experience, simply skip that step and then follow the next one - do not change the order of the steps.

Due to the popularity of *The Wizarding World of Harry Potter* many people head straight to this area early in the day - DON'T! This is what everyone is doing, which means that you end up getting yourself into insanely long queues from the start of the day!

The exception is if you have Early Park Admission into *The Wizarding World of Harry Potter* – then you should explore all of this section of the park during this first 30 minutes, and then use the touring plan.

One Day at Universal Studios Hollywood

Step 1: Be at the park at least 30 minutes before opening. The park regularly opens before the official scheduled opening time. Pick up a park map and show times guide on the way in. These are usually available right by the turnstiles when entering.

Step 2: While everyone else is heading to *The Wizarding of Harry Potter* early in the day, we will walk towards *The Simpsons Ride,* continuing past it and then down the Star Way to the lower lot.

Step 3: Ride *Transformers*.

Step 4: The Lower Lot will still be empty. Ride *Revenge of the Mummy*. This ride may open 30 minutes after park opening. If it is not yet open, follow step 6 first, then return to this step.

Step 5: If may be early in the day to get wet, but this is the best time to experience *Jurassic World: The Ride* before the queues start to build up as it gets warmer. If you have followed this plan, you will have ridden three of the park's star attractions in under 45 minutes. These will get waits of at least 30-60 minutes *each* later in the day.

Step 6: Head back up to the Upper Lot and ride *The Simpsons Ride*.

Step 7: Ride *Despicable Me: Minion Mayhem*. This ride has long waits throughout the day.

Step 8: It is now time to ride

the park's star attraction – the *Universal Studio Tour*. This will take about an hour in total to experience, plus the queue line. If you are feeling hungry, grab a snack to eat while waiting.

Step 9: Have lunch immediately after riding the *Universal Studio Tour*. The park will be at its busiest with long waits for most attractions. We, however, have done almost every major attraction by now.

Step 10: After lunch, you will watch the park's major shows. Check their schedules and see them back to back. These include *Animal Actors, the Special Effects Show* and *WaterWorld*. You will need about two hours to watch them all. If time is short, pick and choose – we would skip *Animal Actors* if we had to choose one.

Step 11: Be sure to schedule in time to watch *Kung Fu Panda* as well. This show that seats a few hundred people every 15 to 20 minutes. The wait time sign for this show never goes below 20 minutes as that is

how long it takes for a cycle of people to see the show. Therefore, if you see a 20-minute wait, chances are you will be in the next show. Note that there are higher than usual wait times for *Kung Fu Panda* after each *WaterWorld* show finishes as many guests enter the queue at once.

Step 12: To be scared, enter *The Walking Dead* maze.

Step 13: Finish off the day with *The Wizarding World of Harry Potter*. Here, you have to play it somewhat by ear. *Ollivanders* and *Harry Potter and the Forbidden Journey* can both get some of the longest waits in the entire park. Do both of these attractions.

If time is short, we would prioritize *Forbidden Journey*. It is the best attraction in the park, in our opinion. *Flight of the Hippogriff* may also be of interested to you – it is a small kids' rollercoaster. If you wish to watch any of the live shows in the Wizarding World, take a look at these too.

Universal Studios Hollywood Park Map

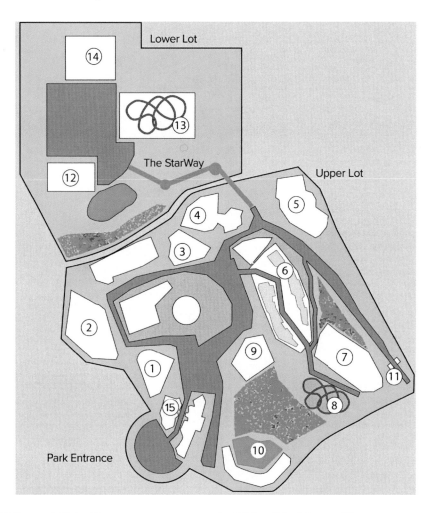

1 - Hollywood Globe Theatre
2 - Despicable Me Minion Mayhem
3 - Universal's Animal Actors
4 - Special Effects Show
5 - The Simpsons Ride
6 - The Wizarding World of Harry Potter: Hogsmeade
7 - Harry Potter and the Forbidden Journey

8 - Flight of the Hippogriff
9 - Dreamworks Theatre Featuring Kung Fu Panda
10 - WaterWorld
11 - Studio Tram Tour
12 - Jurassic World: The Ride
13 - Revenge of the Mummy
14 - Transformers: The Ride-3D

Made in United States
North Haven, CT
28 May 2023

37098628R00027